I0473521

This Journal Belongs To: